# The Four Sacred Seasons

# The Four Sacred Seasons

G. de Purucker

THEOSOPHICAL UNIVERSITY PRESS
PASADENA, CALIFORNIA

Theosophical University Press
Pasadena, California 91109
1979

Copyright © 1979 by Theosophical University Press

All rights including the right of reproduction in whole or in part in any form are reserved under International and Pan American Copyright Conventions.

Library of Congress Catalog Card Number 79-63565

Manufactured in the United States of America

# Contents

|     | *Foreword* | vii |
|-----|------------|-----|
| I   | Winter Solstice | 1 |
| II  | Spring Equinox | 21 |
| III | Summer Solstice | 39 |
| IV  | Autumnal Equinox | 71 |

# Foreword

"Born of the moon, children of the sun, offspring of the stars, and inheritors of the cosmic spaces . . . we and the Boundless are in essence not twain but one." Truly, we humans are wondrously fashioned of the elements of the universe, but we have lost touch with our ancestral heritage and know not where to turn.

Fifty years ago Gottfried de Purucker succeeded Katherine Tingley as international leader of the Theosophical Society, and shortly thereafter instituted regular esoteric studies in order to strengthen the understanding of the members as to the basic goals of the Society, and to awaken them to the deeper dimensions of the spiritual life. These studies were pursued not only by the resident staff, but also by the membership throughout the world.

Two years later, while on his 1931 lecture tour in Europe, Dr. de Purucker announced that henceforth, commencing with the forthcoming Winter Solstice, special quarterly gatherings would be held at headquarters in recognition of the "great spiritual and psychical events" that take place, if the karma is propitious, at the four sacred seasons of the year, namely, the Winter Solstice, Spring Equinox, Summer Solstice, and Autumnal Equinox. The seasonal meetings were subsequently also held in various national centers until World War II. In 1945 they were again held, both at headquarters and abroad, until they were discontinued after the Autumn Equinox of 1950.

For these occasions, Dr. de Purucker gave teachings relevant to the respective season, so that the sublime experiences that the prepared candidate for initiation would one day undergo might, even now, become a living ideal. Key lines of teaching, already treated of in the published literature, on Buddhas and Avatāras and their close relationship to mankind, the circulatory routes of the solar system followed automatically in sleep and death and with full awareness in initiation — these and other salient doctrines are here brought together into an illumined synthesis.

As we read and reflect on the panorama of thought that is opened before our consciousness, we are profoundly moved: we intuitively respond to the stream of altruism flowing in unbroken continuity from the Silent Watcher of our Earth, through the Bodhisattvas and the Christs, on down to us ordinary human beings. And we are assured that if there is the merest stirring in the soul to bend one's energies of heart and head toward lifting the weight of human sorrow, then one already, however unknowingly, places himself in alignment with the beneficent currents of nature. Ultimately, if the aspiration is pure and the will sustained, he may become a conscious helper of the Great Ones in their self-sacrificing labors for mankind.

These seasonal readings, now made public for the first time, are reproduced in toto from the original manuscripts with minimal editing. They are shared after a near half-century in response to the increasing demand for a lucid and informed presentation of what initiation really is.

Grace F. Knoche

February, 1979
Pasadena, California

# I

Winter Solstice

## Winter Solstice

THERE are four turning points of the year: the solstices of winter and summer, and the equinoxes of the spring and of the autumn. The cycle of the year among the ancient peoples was always considered to be a symbol of the life of man or, indeed, of the life of the universe. Birth at the Winter Solstice, the beginning of the year; adolescence — trials and their conquest — at the Spring Equinox; adulthood, full-blown strength and power, at the Summer Solstice, representing a period of initiation when the Great Renunciation is made; and then closing with the Autumnal Equinox, the period of the Great Passing. This cycle of the year likewise symbolizes the training in chelaship.

At the time of the Winter Solstice, two are the main degrees which neophytes or initiants must pass through, to wit, the fourth degree and the seventh or last: the fourth for less great men, although they are great men nonetheless; and the last or seventh initiation, coming but at rare intervals as the ages cycle by, being the birth of the Buddhas and of the Christs.

During the initiation of those individuals of less grandiose spiritual and intellectual capacity than is the human material out of which the Buddhas are born, during this fourth initiation, the postulant is taught to free himself from all the trammels of mind and from the lower four principles of his constitution; and being thus set free he passes along the magnetic channels or circulations of the universe, even to the portals of the Sun, but there and then he stops and returns. Three days usually are the time required for this, and then the man arises a full initiate, but with a realization that ahead of him are still loftier peaks to scale on that lonely path, that still path, that small path, leading to divinity.

As regards the seventh initiation, this occurs in a cycle lasting some 2,160 human years, the time which it takes for a zodiacal sign to pass through a constellation backwards into the next constellation; in other words, what is called among mystics in the Occident the Messianic Cycle. When the planets Mercury and Venus, and Sun and Moon and Earth, are situated in syzygy, then the freed monad of the lofty neophyte can pass along the magnetic pathway through these bodies and continue direct to the heart of the Sun. For fourteen days the man left on Earth is as in a trance, or walks about in a daze, in a quasi-stupor; for the inner part of him, the real part of him, is peregrinating through the spheres. Two weeks later, during the light half of the lunar cycle or month, that is, when the moon stands full, his peregrinating monad returns rapidly as flashing thought along the same pathway by which it ascended to Father Sun, retaking to itself the habiliments which it dropped on each planet as it passed through it: the habiliments of Mercury, the habiliments of Venus, the habiliments of the Moon — of the lunar body, of the lunar orb — and from the Moon the monad returns to the entranced body left behind. Then for a while, shorter or longer according to circumstances, the neophyte's whole being is irradiated with the solar spiritual splendor, and he is a Buddha just "born." All his body is in flaming glory, as it were; and from his head, and from back of his head in especial, as an aureole, there spring forth rays, rays of glory like a crown. It is because of this that crowns in the Occident and diadems in the Hither East were formerly worn by those who had passed through this degree, for verily they are Sons of the Sun, crowned with the solar splendor.

In these initiations the man dies. Initiation is death, death of the lower part of the man; and in actual fact the body dies but is nevertheless held alive, not by the spirit-soul which has flown from it as a butterfly frees itself from its chrysalis, but kept alive by those who are watching and waiting and guarding. It is due to this holding of the bodily triad alive that the peregrinating spirit-soul is enabled finally to return as a bird to its nest, where it recognizes its former bodily home, and is "reborn," but in this case reborn into the same body. During the period of time when the peregrinating monad is absent, whether it be for three days or for fourteen, the excarnate monad has followed the pathways of death literally, but has done so quickly and within the fortnight. In actual fact the process is virtually identic with that followed in the case of excarnation and reincarnation, for it returns to the entranced body along the pathways of rebirth, of reimbodiment, and is, as it were, reborn into the old body instead of into a new one; and thus was it said of such a man in India that he is a *dwija* — as the Brahmans of Āryāvarta put it — a "twice-born" initiate.

This phrase also has one meaning more: one who is reborn from the ashes of the old life, which life is now burnt out and dead. But it has also the deeper significance of which I have spoken. These seventh-degree initiations which occur once during the Messianic Cycle, and which produce the spiritual fruit of a minor Buddha called a Bodhisattva, must not be confused with one of the greatest of initiations known to the human race, that is, those belonging solely to the racial Buddhas. There are in any root-race but two racial Buddhas. But the Bodhisattvas of differing degrees of evolutionary grandeur are very numerous. The cyclical Bodhisattvas as above hinted come, one each, in every Messianic Cycle of 2,160 years, and are usually of an avatāric character.

There are cases where neophytes fail, yet those who fail have another chance in other lives; but the penalty for failure in this life is either death or madness, and the penalty is very just. Solemn indeed are the warnings given to those who would fly like the birds into the ethers of the inner worlds and follow the tracks of those who have preceded them along the circulations of the universe.

When you look up at the starry night or

during the daytime raise your eyes and look at the splendor of Father Sun shining in the blue vault of midday, how empty the spacial expanse seems to be — how seeming vacuous, how seeming void! Astronomers tell us that the earth is a sphere poised in the void, in the ether, free except for the gravitational attraction of the sun, and that the earth is following its pathway, its orbit, around the sun not otherwise than gravitationally attached thereto; in short, that "space" is emptiness. Ay, indeed, space, mystically speaking, is *śūnyatā*, "emptiness" in its esoteric significance, but by no means "emptiness" as Occidental astronomers understand it; for verily the space which we look at, which our physical eyes think they see — or don't see — is substance so dense, so concrete, that no human conception can give any clear idea thereof to the brain-mind otherwise than by mathematics.

One physicist-astronomer, J. J. Thomson, some years ago calculated that the ether of space was two thousand million times denser than lead. This revoices an old doctrine; but remember that the proper manner of expressing this fact all depends upon the way in which we look at it. We have eyes evolved to sense, to pierce, the matter of *our* sphere, and we see what seems to us to be vacuity, emptiness; but actually that seeming vacuity or emptiness is absolutely full, is, in fact, a plenum, a pleroma, full of worlds and spheres and planes, full of hierarchies, of evolving entities on these worlds and spheres and planes.

Please try clearly to grasp this idea. Our entire *sūrya*-system, our entire solar system, called the Egg of Brahmā, may be looked at from one very true standpoint as an enormous ovoid aggregate body poised in space; and were some astronomer on some distant globe in the stellar deeps to see our Egg of Brahmā, and were he to see it from the proper superior plane or world, our entire solar system would appear to him as an ovoid body of light — as an egg-shaped irresolvable nebula. This would include all the "emptiness" that we see, or think we see, the emptiness so called, and therefore would include all our solar world of the Egg of Brahmā, from the very heart of Father Sun to beyond the confines of what astronomers call the farthermost planets.

The Egg of Brahmā is composed of concentric spheres centered in the Sun, and each one of these spheres is a cosmic world. Its heart — the heart of each one of them — is the Sun. The world or sphere of our Earth is one such, and surrounds the Sun as a sphere of dense substance, and the nucleus in this sphere or egg, for such it is, is what we commonly call our Earth. Such also is the sphere of Mercury, such is the sphere of Venus, such is the sphere of Mars, also of Jupiter, also of Saturn; yes, and of Uranus too — but remember that Uranus belongs not to our own system of sacred worlds, although it belongs to our Egg of Brahmā.

In this connection note well that although any concentric sphere such as that of our Earth, or that of Jupiter, or that of Mercury, is de facto such an Egg or Sphere of Brahmā, yet the nucleus of each such sphere or planet, if seen in motion from another plane, would appear to be a wave or ripple advancing steadily in and around a solid or semisolid zone or belt; this zone or belt actually being what we call on our plane the locus of the orbit of such planetary body as of Earth, or of Jupiter, or of Mercury. The meaning of this again is that a planetary orbit, such as that of Earth seen from another plane, is an actual belt or zone surrounding the Sun, being the pathway, so to speak, of the nucleus which in this zone can be considered in movement as a ripple or wave moving steadily around this belt, or zone, or ring. From what has just been said, it becomes immediately obvious that what we call a planet can be properly viewed from three different planes of vision, as three different things: first, as a globe such as we on this plane see it; second, from another plane as a wave or ripple, circularly advancing in and following the course of an annular zone or belt surrounding the Sun; and third, as a concentric sphere, or rather spheroid, or egg, with its center at the heart of the Sun.

These concentric worlds or spheres are in constant circular movement of revolution around the heart of the Sun, the spheres within each other somewhat like the skins of an onion, and yet each one is formed of different matters in a sense, of matters in a different state from the matters of the other spheres, and hence they pass through each other as easily as if the others did not exist. Thus it is that our eye can see some of the stellar bodies lying beyond the orbits of Mars and of Jupiter and of Saturn. All we see of the stellar host outside of our Egg of Brahmā happens to be those particular stars or suns which, by reason of their having attained the same degree of material evolution whereon we ourselves now stand and where our physical sun is, therefore are visible to our organs of sight. Were we living on another plane, our vision could not penetrate the respective matters, otherwise the orbits or spheres, of Mars or Jupiter or of Saturn. These three planets alone hide billions and billions and billions of suns that we during our present manvantara or world-cycle cannot ever see. Some day in the far distant future, as evolution works on the matter of our world-sphere, we shall see some of the rājā-suns now hid by these three planets — by the spheres of these three planets, for the planets and their respective spheres are really the same. It is precisely because the Egg of Brahmā is substantial throughout, and that interplanetary space is therefore substantial throughout, that light belonging to this fourth cosmic plane can pass from stars to us.

In speaking of these concentric spheres, please remember also that a proper conception of the structure and characteristics of the Egg of Brahmā must include a realization of the significant fact that there are many more planetary concentric spheres than those of the eight or nine or ten planets known to Occidental astronomy. There are scores of planets in the solar system which are utterly invisible by means of any astronomical instrument or apparatus, and furthermore, and still more important, there are numbers of these concentric spheres which belong to entirely other planes of the cosmos, and each one of these invisible concentric spheres, which are in some cases superior and in some cases inferior to our plane, is as fully inhabited with its multifarious hosts of beings as our own plane is. Each plane has its own hierarchies of inhabitants, its own inhabited worlds with their dwellers, with their countries, with their mountains, and seas, and lakes, and dwellings, and whatnot, even as our Earth has.

These concentric world-spheres considered as a whole were the crystalline spheres of the ancients, which astronomers have so grossly misunderstood, and therefore have so much derided. What indeed did these words mean: "crystalline spheres"? The meaning was, spheres of which the center was the Sun and which were transparent to our eyesight. Just as glass is very dense and yet is transparent to our eyesight, so are the ethers of our fourth cosmic plane very dense and yet transparent to us. To the inhabitants of Earth viewing the phenomena of the solar system from the Earth, the entire system of concentric spheres, due to the Earth's rotation, seems to revolve around the Earth, and hence arises the geocentric way of looking at the apparent movements of the planets and the Sun, Moon, and stars. All things in universal nature are repetitive in structure and in action. The small mirrors the great, and the great reproduces itself in the small, for verily the twain are one.

Furthermore, on account of the magnetic structure and action of the twelve globes of our planetary chain, our Earth has magnetic bipolar action of twelve different kinds; one such polar pair is known to scientists, the others unknown. Our Egg of Brahmā, our solar system, as a whole, likewise has twelve magnetic bipolar courses or what in short are called magnetic poles, and each one of these twelve poles has its locus in one of the twelve constellations of the zodiac — or rather the twelve constellations of the zodiac are the loci of the twelve poles of the zodiacal period. The wheel of life with its twelve spokes runs on forever.

Thus it is that a human being can be a son of the Sun. Thus it is that a human being can ascend along the magnetic pathways from Earth to Moon, from Moon to Venus, from Venus to Mercury, from Mercury to the heart of Father Sun — and return. On the journey outwards, certain sheaths or integuments of the peregrinating monad are dropped at each planetary station. Dust to dust on Earth. The lunar body is cast off and abandoned in the valleys of the Moon. On Venus, habiliments of Venusian character are cast aside also; and so is it likewise on Mercury. Then the solar portion of us is ingathered into its own heart. The peregrinating monad on its return journey leaves the Sun after reassuming its own solar sheath. It enters the sphere of Mercury, gathers up there the garments that it previously had cast aside, assumes these, and then passes to Venus, reclothes itself with what it had there previously laid down, then enters the unholy sphere of the Moon, and in its dark valleys picks up its former lunar body, and thence is borne to Earth on the lunar rays when the Moon is full. Dust to dust, Moon to Moon, Venus to Venus, Mercury to Mercury, Sun to Sun!

Initiation is the becoming, by self-conscious experience, temporarily at one with other worlds and planes, and the various degrees of initiation mark the various stages of advancement or of ability to do this. As the initiations progress in grandeur, so does the spirit-soul of the initiant penetrate deeper and deeper into the invisible worlds and spheres. One must become fully cognizant of all the secrets of the solar egg before one can become a divinity in that solar egg, taking a part, self-conscious and deliberate, in the cosmic labor.

Prepare yourselves continually, for every day is a new chance, is a new doorway, a new opportunity. Lose not the days of your lives, for the time will come, fatally come, when it will be your turn to undertake this sublimest of adventures. Glorious beyond words to express will be the reward if you succeed. Therefore practice, practice continuously your will. Open your heart more and more. Remember the divinity at your inmost, the inmost divinity of you, the heart of you, the core of you. Love others, for these others are yourself. Forgive them, for in so doing you forgive yourself. Help them, for in so doing you strengthen yourself. Hate them, and in so doing you prepare your own feet to travel to the Pit, for in so doing you hate yourself. Turn your backs on the Pit, and turn your faces to the Sun!

# II

# Spring Equinox

# Spring Equinox

LET US now turn to the spring equinoctial initiatory cycle. Concerning this there is a doctrine which is both wonderful and strange, and which is based on the operations of Mother Nature herself. It should be remembered that this phrase Mother Nature, when used with its esoteric significancy, includes not only the physical shell of the universe surrounding us, of which we know the existence through our imperfect senses of report, but also more particularly includes the vast and indeed frontierless realms of the spaces of space.

This strange and wonderful doctrine sets forth that the great initiatory adventure upon which the lofty initiant enters at the time of the Spring Equinox is a copy, a duplication, a repetitive event, in our own small human sphere of what actually occurs at cosmical time intervals among the gods. The initiations which take place even today with more or less uninterrupted regularity at the time of the Spring Equinox include, not only the passing through trials and an ultimate resurrection from the personal man of the god within and an ascension into the spiritual realms, at least for a time, of the initiant's percipient consciousness, but includes also what it has been customary to call in Occidental literature dealing with this theme the descent of the neophyte-initiant, however grand his spiritual stature may be, into the Underworld, into those very real but to us utterly invisible realms of space which have their being in cosmic reaches still more material than our gross sphere of physical māyāvi-substance.

It would be wrong to consider this Underworld as belonging exclusively to what has been called in theosophical literature the Eighth Sphere, otherwise the Planet of Death, although indeed the Eighth Sphere must be visited by the percipient consciousness peregrinating at the time.

We have thus, then, a picture of the initiation of the Spring Equinox as a phase of the general initiatory cycle, this phase consisting of severe and searching trials of spiritual and intellectual and psychical as well as astral tests on the one hand, and on the other hand as likewise comprising a descent into spheres never traversed in the ordinary course of their development by the peregrinating monads of average human beings, once these monads have begun to manifest in the human stage.

This strange and mysterious doctrine as thus briefly outlined sets forth that on this our Earth, on this holy and solemn occasion, there occurs a repetition or a duplication of what at certain intervals takes place among the divinities. Just as at certain times in the progress of cosmic destiny a certain divinity leaves its own luminous realms in order to "descend," or more accurately to transfer a portion of its own divine essence, into the world of men for the purpose of aiding and helping erring mankind, so exactly does the neophyte-initiant descend or transfer his percipient consciousness into the Underworld in order to learn and also to help the denizens of those gloomy spheres. What the gods from their lofty height do in this connection to help us, this do likewise these great men in spheres below our own.

One may well ask oneself, as one ponders deeply over this profound teaching and begins to sense its extraordinary and puzzling paradoxes, why it is that a divinity at any time should "descend," or project a portion of its essence, into our sphere which it had long aeons ago left behind in its evolutionary progress. The explanation lies in other teachings concerning the nature of our cosmical solar system, as viewed from the spiritual standpoint. We learn that even the gods themselves are under the sway of almighty destiny, that even they in their own lofty spheres make and unmake karma, and begin, and end after bringing to their completion, works of far-reaching influence on the cosmical spaces, and that a certain portion of these divine activities must of necessity reach to and influence most deeply the spheres of men.

When the student of esotericism understands the profound philosophical import of the teachings concerning the real meaning of the triad of Hindu deities called Brahmā, Vishnu, and Śiva, he will come to understand why these amazing events just spoken of take place. As Brahmā is the evolver and the producer, and as Vishnu is the sustainer and upholder, so is Śiva, who is the particular patron of esotericists, the regenerator because of being the resolver.

To look upon this triad of divinities in the solar system in the manner in which the Hindu exoteric literary works set them forth is entirely to lose the real meaning and the reach of the esoteric teaching concerning them. The three are three individuals indeed, and yet they are one, very much as evolution and involution are twain and yet are essentially one, because nothing can evolve what is within itself before that within has been involved into it. Thus there can be no Brahmā or evolver or producer unless the regenerator or resolver in a past cosmic period had already involved the seeds of the universe later to be evolved or produced. Nor could there be any manvantara or sustained course of cosmic life and evolution unless due to the incessant and continuous influence of the sustainer, upholder, and preserver.

Now, then, these three spiritual-divine energies in the solar system, which are distinctly three and yet one in essence, verily are the higher triad of the septenary belonging to the ten principles of our solar cosmos, and therefore exist and work in their sublimity in what is to us utter silence and darkness, because of being the higher three of the solar system's septenary of worlds of life-energy-consciousness.

From time to time, governed strictly by the karma of the solar system, there arises an impulse in the bosom of Mahā-Vishnu to manifest a portion of itself, this portion being a divinity; and this impulse or super-spiritual urge cannot ever be denied or set aside. This impulse furthermore has a technical name in esoteric teaching. It is called *bīja,* meaning "seed" or, more accurately perhaps, *avatāra-bīja* — the cosmic seed of the Avatāras.

The Avatāras appear on Earth at intervals when the spiritual energies are running low amongst us, and the forces of matter are surging in turbulent waves ever higher. It is as if there were a spiritual psychomagnetic strain in the structure of the solar system, resulting in a spiritual-electric discharge of a spiritual energy, something like lightning on earth, this discharge being popularly called the "descent" of the Avatāra, thus preserving the stability and the equilibrium of things. Just so, then, in our world, is it in the cases of these great men, these sublime neophyte-initiants, who during the course of their initiation "descend" into the Underworld for the sake of bringing a spiritual light to the beings inchained in the darkness of those gloomy spheres — spheres which to us seem realms of gloom only because we are higher than they.

So closely is all nature knitted together, so intimately and intricately are the strands of the web of life woven, that all nature must be considered as one vast organism; and when there is a lack of some element-energy in any part of the cosmic body, there is an impulse or urge from other parts, possessing this lacking element-energy in abundance, towards the place where such lack exists, and a consequent passage or peregrination or transference of the lacking element-energy to its destination in order that stability and equilibrium of the cosmical structure may be reestablished or maintained.

The initiation periods do not take place by hap or by hazard, nor are they governed by the mere wish or will of human beings, however grand, however sublime, but take place strictly according to the working of the spiritual cosmic magnetisms of the universe. In consequence, the grand neophyte-initiants enter upon their trials and make their journeys into the Underworld because for the time being they are become utterly obedient servants of the law of the universe, and therefore can hardly do otherwise.

From what has been said, therefore, it becomes immediately obvious how grandly does nature's heart beat throughout with compassionate pulse; for what men in their feebleness of speech describe by such phrases as the reestablishing of disturbed equilibrium, or the maintenance of cosmic stability, is but a poor way of expressing the fact of the automatic operation of the cosmic life in restoring the cosmic harmonies, in the readjustment of the cosmic energies, all under the governance and control of the ineffably grand heart of life-consciousness which beats unceasingly and without pause or surcease to the very end of the solar manvantara.

Hence it is that the Spring Equinox in particular and the Avatāras are associated in both human thought and in cosmic actuality. Bear in mind that three are the general cases or general instances in which there occur descents or avatāric manifestations of spiritual energies into human existence as extraordinarily powerful motors. One is that of the Avatāras produced by influence of the *bīja* in Mahā-Vishnu; the second is the case of the Buddhas; and the third is that occurring at rare intervals among human beings who are neither Avatāras nor Buddhas. Mark well that the Avatāra is the descent of the influence, or of a portion, of a divinity through a loaned intermediate bodhisattvic psychological apparatus in order to manifest in human life in a pure human body. The Buddhas incarnate their own spiritual-divine influences, in each case emanating from the Buddha's own inner god, and do this through the entire term of their work in the world of men; and they manifest these spiritual powers in purposes and works of indescribably lofty benevolence and far-reaching beneficence.

The cases of the rare humans who, being

neither Avatāras nor Buddhas, from time to time imbody or become the dwelling places of spiritual-divine rays, are those unusual men or women who, because of a line of karma which is singularly free from crippling and embarrassing shackles of personality, are able to transmit a ray from the higher triads of themselves. This ray penetrates into and sets on fire with its holy flame the brain-mind and emotional apparatus of such men and women.

The cases of these unusual human beings can be instanced or demonstrated by men and women whose entire existence seems to show a spiritual and intellectual power exceeding by far that of the average run of men, and yet they are human beings only. They may, for instance, be great and nobleminded poets with the seer's vision; they may again be great and nobleminded artists, philosophers, humanitarians, or statesmen; but they are men and men only. They are neither Avatāras on the one hand, nor Buddhas on the other hand, and their existence is so well known in the various world religions that they have been called by various names, such as saints or holy men, or by other similar titles.

Although these three classes manifesting spiritual-divine rays — so different as among themselves — are the three instances in which the divine-spiritual manifests in the human sphere, it must be particularly noticed that the originating impulse or urge in all these three classes takes its rise in the mysterious *bīja* existing and working from dawn to twilight of a cosmic manvantara in the bosom of Mahā-Vishnu.

As a last thought in this connection, mark well that there are Avatāras also of Mahā-Śiva, just as well as there are Avatāras of Vishnu, the sustainer of the solar universe; and it is these Avatāras of Mahā-Śiva, the solar regenerator, which produce perhaps the most widespread and world-shaking effects in the sphere of men.

The duty of some of the Avatāras, their characteristic or swabhāva, is to preserve and sustain all that is spiritual, noble, good, lofty, and holy; whereas the work of other Avatāras is to regenerate, to make over anew, to bring forth from the womb of destiny what is waiting to come to birth. Hence it is that the work of the Śiva-influence has often and always stupidly been called destruction. The profound philosophy of the process has not been grasped by either Occidental or Oriental scholars; but it is obvious that there are times, brought about by the whirling wheel of life, when evil in the course of destiny must be overthrown, when structures and works which have outlasted their times must be destroyed from the foundations up, in order that a newer building and a grander and loftier structure, both spiritually and materially speaking, shall be raised.

Difficult indeed is the theme of thought upon which I have embarked, and I feel urged to utter a word of warning that one not leap to points of conclusion on the supposition that one has grasped the full import of the meaning of the wonderful doctrine that I have so briefly outlined. Remember that the entire solar universe is one vast organism, quivering and palpitating with life throughout all its reaches, and that what men call spirit or what men call matter are but two phases or two aspects or two events of the onrushing, or the onsweeping, of the cosmic life-consciousness-substance working out its incomprehensibly sublime destiny.

Thus it is that our entire solar system can be viewed from two aspects: one as a cosmic body of spheres builded of the fabric of the cosmic consciousness; and from the other aspect it can be looked upon as an amazingly and most intricately intertwined web of spheres existing on many planes, but all under the dominance, and existing within the limits, of our cosmic divinity. Hence every atom is quivering with life, and is an imbodied consciousness center, which we call a monad, and the only difference between atom and god, between the hosts of darkness and the hosts of light, is one of evolutionary unfoldment.

Finally, let us try to understand somewhat of the meaning of the experiences, so full of mystery and danger, that certain ones, more evolved than we, are now undergoing.

# Summer Solstice

## Summer Solstice

WE NOW celebrate the third of the great spiritual and psychical events of the esoteric year, the initiation cycle centering in the Summer Solstice; we celebrate in teaching and by spiritual and intellectual suggestion the actual events of the initiations which take place at this time elsewhere on the surface of the globe.

It is a most suggestive thought, and one that we should carry with us always — each one of us as his or her most prized ideal — that anyone belonging to the outer ring of the mystic Body can, if he or she so will, some day pass from the outer ring to an inner ring, and from that inner ring to one still nearer the center; and so on, until finally, if the disciple prevail in the conquest of self and in the enlargement of consciousness, he shall one day reach the center, and thence by his own will and act be swept into the initiatory life-currents which will bear him on the mystic pilgrimage, on the esoteric round of experience, and return a willing and self-conscious renouncer of what he knows he can get, but which he refuses in order to remain and to help the world as one of the stones in the Guardian Wall surrounding humanity.

You will remember that the mystic year contains four seasonal points, and that these four seasons in their cycle are symbolic of the four chief events of progress of initiation: first, that of the Winter Solstice, which event is also called the Great Birth, when the aspirant brings to birth the god within him and for a time at least becomes temporarily at one therewith in consciousness and in feeling; a birth which indeed is the birth of the inner Buddha born of the spiritual solar splendor, or the birth of the mystic Christos.

Then, second, comes the period or event of esoteric adolescence at the Spring Equinox, when in the full flush of the victory gained at the Winter Solstice, and with the marvelous inner strength and power that come to one who has thus achieved, the aspirant enters upon the greatest temptation, except one, known to human beings, and prevails; and this event may be called the Great Temptation. With this initiation at the time of the Spring Equinox the Avatāras are particularly concerned, forming as they do one of the lines of activity — a god-line, in fact — of the Hierarchy of Compassion and Splendor, although the Avatāras are outside the circle of temptation except insofar as concerns the human portion of them.

Then, third, comes the event of the Summer Solstice, at which time the neophyte or aspirant must undergo, and successfully prevail over, the greatest temptation known to man just referred to; and if he so prevail, which means the renouncing of all chance of individual progress for the sake of becoming one of the Saviors of the world, he then takes his position as one of the stones in the

Guardian Wall. Thereafter he dedicates his life to the service of the world, without thought of guerdon or of individual progress — it may be for aeons — sacrificing himself spiritually in the service of all that lives. For this reason the initiation at this season of the year has been called the Great Renunciation.

Then, finally, comes the fourth and last period of the cycling mystical year, the event of the Autumnal Equinox, which perhaps is the most sublime, but which actually is not as holy as the initiation which we are now commemorating; because in the initiation of the Autumnal Equinox the neophyte or aspirant passes beyond the portals of irrevocable death, and returns among men no more. One line of this activity, lofty and spiritual but yet not the line of the Hierarchy of Splendor and Compassion, is that followed by the Pratyeka Buddhas. Aeons will pass before these Pratyeka Buddhas reawaken to take up anew the evolutionary journey, the evolutionary pilgrimage.

The Autumnal Equinox is likewise straitly

and closely related to the investigation, during the rites and trials of the neophyte, of the many and varied and intricate mysteries connected with death. For these and for other reasons it has been called the Great Passing.

Children of the Sun and Offspring of the Stars: Has it ever occurred to you to ask yourselves why it is that the stars glitter in the violet dome of night; why our sun shines with unceasing glory, pouring forth through aeons after aeons its own substance of light and life and energy; and why, on the other hand, such vast stretches and realms of nature are sunken in apparently cold and crystalline rigidity: asleep, dormant, seemingly unmoving, although indeed pervaded everywhere and throughout (so that not even an atom is deprived of it) by the all-permeant life and consciousness of the Boundless? Have you ever wondered why these two great contrasts exist in the manifested universe — on the one side, light and movement, activity and power, offspring of divinity and of the spiritual energies; and on the other side, relative immobility, rigidity, crystalline somnolence, and the realms of cold and spiritual sleep?

If you have not asked yourselves these questions, you have not yet really awakened; your spiritual souls are not yet stirring consciously within you, and you are asleep, you are dormant. It is the beasts that ask themselves no such questions as these, as they live within the restricted bounds of their limited consciousness, for it is a consciousness of feeling and of reaction to feeling only, without the divine fire of self-conscious thought, and without that inquisitive intelligence, that thirst for light and knowledge, which characterize man as a son of the Sun and as an offspring of a stellar parent.

Spirit on one side and matter on the other, conscious life on one side and relative immobility and somnolence of consciousness on the other. As we look upon tenfold nature and consider her activities, we realize that we can figurate the situation as a vast army of the sons of light working upon dark and sleeping matter, the sons of light existing in their imbodiments between two poles, both of which to our present human consciousness seem to be impenetrable realms of being. What are these two poles? One is the pole of matter, but the other is the pole of spirit which, because of its incomprehensible brilliance and power, is so far beyond all our intellectual conception or loftiest ideation that it seems as impenetrable to understanding as does the nether pole just spoken of, also apparently dark and incomprehensible.

The reason why nature is thus divided in twain to the understanding of us humans is because we observe on one side the hosts of light, and on the other side the hosts of matter; and yet both fundamentally are one, the difference being that the hosts of light are entities more or less progressed towards the pole of spirit, and the hosts of darkness are ruled by the *māmo-chohans;* as, indeed, the light side is ruled by the Hierarchies of Splendor consisting of *dhyāni-chohans* in ever increasing ranges of glory, ascending along the ladder of life beyond the reach of our utmost vision, strain we it upwards as we may. These two, nature's dark side and her light side, are the two eternal pathways, eternal because of being mighty nature herself. We may speak of the upper or light side as being that of the Hierarchies of Compassion, and the lower or dark side as being that of the Hierarchies of Matter; yet both sides are eternally evolving upwards in everlasting progress. After all, these are but two modes of life, for fundamentally the two are one.

As said a great sage and seer of the Far Orient, Lao-tse, when speaking of the Tao:

> Its upper part is not bright, and its lower part is not dark. Unceasing in action, nevertheless it cannot ever be named, but from action returns again to the spiritual Void. We may call it the form of the formless, the image of the imageless, the fleeting and the indeterminable [and yet it is the ever-enduring]. Go you before it, you cannot see its face; go you behind it, you cannot see its back. . . .

Without a name by which it may rightfully be called, it is the origin of the spheres celestial and the spheres material. When it has a name men call it the Eternal Mother of all things. Only he who is constantly free from earthly passions can understand its divine essence; but he whose mind is clogged and blinded by passions can see no more than its outer form. Yet these two, the spiritual and the material, though we call them by different names, in their origin are identically one and identically the same. This sameness is a wondrous mystery, the mystery of mysteries. Understanding this mystery is the portal of all initiation.\*

Children of the Sun, Offspring of the Stars: Are you like the blind unreasoning beast that has no divine curiosity for wisdom and knowledge and love? Or are you becoming like unto the sages and the seers of the ages, who see in all that surrounds them, in every minutest as well as in every greatest

---

\*Passages from the *Tao-te ching* paraphrased from Lionel Giles's translation.

thing or event, a key to a cosmic riddle? Think, and pause a moment over the thought. When you consider the glittering orbs above us and our own glorious daystar whom we call Father Sun, has it never occurred to you that these very stars are manifestations of the Hierarchy of Compassion, bringing light and life and love and wisdom into the dark realms of nature's material spheres? Verily it is so!

Every sun that we discern in the midnight sky, every human creature, every dhyāni-chohan whose presence we may instinctively feel, is not only an evolving and progressing entity — especially in the cases of the stars and of the gods — but is also an entity which, motivated by celestial love and wisdom divine, each one in accordance with its own karmic powers and to the extent that it may, has halted on its path or advances slowly on its path, in order to give help to the multitudes and hosts of less progressed entities trailing along behind.

Thus a star, our sun for instance, is not

only an evolving god in its divine and spiritual and intellectual and psychical and astral aspects, but is also bending towards us from its celestial throne as it were, and thus appears in our own material realms helping us, giving us light, urging us upwards.

These are no merely vain words of an empty poesy, but are suggestive truth. Everywhere around us nature proclaims law, order, regularity, a succession of event ever following event as beings and things are swept along through the ages on the vast bosom of the river of lives; and all this is the work of the Hierarchy of Splendor and Compassion, of which we in our own humble way form on this earth the outmost circle or sphere. It is the same impulse which sways the gods and the Silent Watchers and the starry beings to help those less progressed, that sways the hearts of the Buddhas of Compassion, and of the Masters of Wisdom and Peace and of their chelas, to take the initiation of the Great Renunciation, thus copying in our human realm what takes place in sublime degree among the divinities. An Avatāra is but an exceptional case of a peculiar kind, exemplifying the rule of which the Buddhas are the still nobler and outstanding examples of the general case.

Little do men know of the immense love, the divine impulses of compassion, which sway the souls of those who make the Great Renunciation, giving up all hope of personal evolutionary progress, it may be for aeons to come, in order to remain on earth to help their fellows and in the service of the world. Unrecognized, unthanked, ever silent, ever compassionate, ever filled with holy peace, they work steadily on, watching others go past them as the slowly moving river of lives sweeps along in unending flow. There they stand like pillars of light, these great and noble ones. Although they know that some day their reward shall come, a reward beyond all human understanding, nevertheless there they remain through the ages without thinking of their reward, and endure and endure and endure.

Men in the world have no cognizance whatsoever of the mighty hands and powerful wills which hold back certain cosmic forces and elements, lest these forces and elements ravage men because of the ignorant stupidity and blind willfulness of men in invoking, through their selfish emotions and thoughts, cosmic powers of which they actually have no real consciousness. Because these Great Ones are the protecting shields of mankind, therefore are they called the Guardian Wall.

Every man or woman who does a generous, unselfish, and compassionate act is, by the same token and insofar as the compassionate impulse and act extend, a member of the Hierarchy of Compassion and Splendor. Every man or woman who commits an act of selfishness or who follows blindly and solely an impulse of the matter side of himself or of herself is, by the same token and insofar as the impulse and act extend, acting under the influence of the somber and unholy powers of the material world whose chiefs are the dread māmo-chohans presiding at the pralayas. Every man or woman who does a selfish, evil, or ignoble act, in very truth is taking a stride backwards and is, let us say in passing, by just so much hindering the forward progress of his fellows; for we are all knitted inseparably together into one web of life, into one living organic union.

How beautiful are they upon whose foreheads shines the light eternal, the light of everlasting peace, the light of wisdom, and the illumination of deathless love! They are growing, and growing rapidly, stimulated by the radiant light which pours forth from within the deeps of their own spiritual being. How blessed is their peace, how unspeakably great their happiness, how calm, how majestic, do they appear! What wonderful strength also are they gaining by each such noble thought, by each such noble act! Men and women who incarnate this spirit of selfless devotion, in however small a degree, are preparing themselves for a future time when they in turn will stand at the door and knock, seeking, asking for, demanding, and demanding with the innate right of embryo gods, this initiation of the Great Renunciation; and then they will find their place as self-conscious workers in the Hierarchy of Compassion and Splendor.

As Lao-tse again says in this connection, when speaking of the Tao, which is at once the cosmic organism in its divine side and the timeless splendor within the aspirant's own breast: "The entire world of men will flock eagerly to him who holds within himself the mighty form and power of Tao. They will come and receive no hurt, but will find rest, peace, tranquillity, and wisdom."

In speaking again of the practical ethics of him who has already made the Great Renunciation and has passed through the holy rites, the great Chinese Master continues:

> He that is empty shall be filled; he that is worn out shall be renewed; he who has little shall have all; he who thinks he has much shall go astray. Therefore the sage embraces in thought the cosmic unity, and thereby be-

comes a model for all under heaven. He is free from self-display, therefore he shines forth; free from self-assertion, therefore he is distinguished; free from self-glorification, therefore he is glorified; free from self-exaltation, therefore he rises above all. Inasmuch as he never strives with others, there is no one in the world who strives with him.

And further, the same sage and seer, in his paradoxes, taught as follows:

> Therefore the sage, wishing to be above the people, must by his words put himself below the people. Desiring to be ever nobler than the multitude, he must put himself modestly behind them and at their service. In this way, though he has his natural place above them, the people do not feel his weight; though he has his natural place before them, they do not resent it. Therefore all mankind delight to exalt him, and weary of him not.
>
> The sage expects no recognition for what he does; he achieves merit but does not take it to himself; . . . I have three precious things which I hold fast and prize above all. The

first is gentleness; the second is frugality; the third is proper humility, which keeps me from putting myself before others. Be gentle, and then you can be bold. Be frugal, and then you can be most liberal. Avoid putting yourself before others, and you naturally become a leader among men.

But in the present day men cast off gentleness, and are all for being bold. They spurn frugality, and retain only extravagance; they discard proper humility, and aim only at being the first. Therefore they shall surely perish.

It must never for a moment be supposed that the Great Renunciation implies an abandonment of any single part of the manifested universe in order that the neophyte or aspirant may devote himself only to following the sole pathway of light. This in itself is a subtly spiritual selfishness which, let men say what they may, is the spirit governing the career of the Pratyeka Buddhas. It is necessary for the neophyte or chela who desires to pass through even the first gateway of the initiation leading to the Great Renunciation to understand that instead of abandoning the world he remains within it, in order, as he grows greater and stronger, wiser and loftier, to serve ever more largely in the cause of all things that are.

The slightest tinge of individual yearning for personal advancement will bar the doors fast against him, for the very core of this initiation is utter self-renunciation. The effort is indeed a titan's labor, for not only must the personal nature be washed clean, but must be utterly transmuted, as far as is compatible with existence in these realms, into becoming a channel or vehicle or mediator between all above the neophyte and all below him and less than he. He must, in consequence, be tested in every fiber of his being before he can even raise his heart to dare the greater trials which will lead him first into the gloom of the regions of the Underworld — for he must prevail or fail; and later, when his utterly pure heart and indomitable will have carried him safely out of these, he must be tested in loftier spheres, so that no yearning hunger for more light for himself and for communion with the divinities for his own grace can entice him away from his self-chosen path.

The path of the Pratyeka Buddha, after all, is a relatively easy one by comparison with the way of the one who has chosen the Great Renunciation; but oh, how inexpressibly beautiful and sublime is the guerdon that comes to the latter in the far distant future when, his work once done, fully accomplished, like the butterfly he frees himself from the chrysalis and, taking wing into the ambient ether where the gods abide, he becomes at one with them, self-consciously a collaborator with them in the cosmic work. But aeons will pass before this stage shall be reached, aeons upon aeons of remaining in our realms of imperfection and often of strife and pain. But to the one who has made the Great Renunciation there is a joy in the heart which passeth all understanding, the joy of helping and of raising and of leading others up the stairway of life. Power becomes his;

faculties hitherto but partly recognized and perhaps unknown develop within him; he becomes cognizant of mysteries of which in the earlier stages of his growth he had but the faintest adumbration, if indeed any intuition of them at all; and the reason is that the farther he advances in his progress the more perfectly, the more completely, the more entirely, does he become a self-conscious mediator of the wisdom and love of the hierarchies above him, who now can work through him as a perfect instrument, willing, self-sacrificing, joyful, strong, and fully capable.

For him no more is there Dead Sea fruit which turns to ashes in the mouth; for him sorrow and pain as men know them have evanished away. He has come to make his own the world's great sorrow and pain; but, marvelous paradox, the unspeakable peace and bliss that are his because he is an utterly unselfish helper transmute the world's sorrow and pain into the greater light and peace of the splendor above and within him. He becomes at one with universal nature, and instinctively works with her in all her labors; and because of this, nature recognizes him as her master and makes obeisance unto him.

There are many grades of those who take the path of the Great Renunciation: there are, first, the loftiest ones, the very gods themselves who lean from their azure thrones, so to speak, and who communicate with those of the same hierarchy but who are less than they. There are innumerable grades still lower down; there are the Buddhas of Compassion; there are the Masters of Wisdom and Peace; there are the high chelas; there are the chelas of lower degree; and there are even ordinary men and women who feel within themselves the upsurging force of the mighty fire of compassionate love which, at times at least, fills their hearts with its flame. Celestial Buddhas, Dhyāni-buddhas, Mānushya-buddhas, Bodhisattvas, Masters, chelas, inferior chelas, and great and noble men and women — there in brief is the line or ladder of being which forms the Order of Compassion.

As the chela advances into masterhood, as the Master becomes the Bodhisattva, and as the Bodhisattva develops into the Buddha, and so forth, there is a growing self-conscious realization that every individual of this Hierarchy of Compassion and Splendor is the vehicle or mediator of a divine entity which works through him as its human channel; and in the seventh initiation, although nothing more here can be said of that last and greatest of rites, the initiant comes face to face, it may be for a brief instant or even for months or possibly years, with this inspiring and overshadowing divine entity.

It must never be supposed that the Great Renunciation implies that, once taken, this debars one from further initiation. The Great Renunciation implies, rather, that the entity so devoting himself consecrates himself to a series of further and ever loftier initiations, but with the sole and single purpose of rendering himself ever more fit for transmitting the divine light to others less advanced than he, and for that purpose alone.

The Great Renunciation is also an initiation having many degrees, for the Silent Watcher of whatever grade is the first exemplar and outstanding type of one who sits on the threshold of knowledge absolute and of unspeakable peace, and yet enters not but remains before the last and greatest holy of holies in order that those less developed may have a link with the highest.

Every higher grade entered into during the long cycle of initiation before man becomes a Bodhisattva is an awakening within the neophyte of a new plane of consciousness and the consequent coming into lofty personal relation with the different powers and forces and even entities that belong to each plane as they are attained, the one after the other. Initiation is not something which is added unto the growing and expanding consciousness of the neophyte, as brick is added to brick in building a wall; but the steps of initiation represent, each one, a quickening of the evolutionary process. In other words, initiation in every instance and throughout time is the bringing out or forth into manifested activity of what already exists within the individual. This thought is so important that I must ask you to pause upon it and to ponder it well. You will at once realize that no initiation can possibly take place merely by request or by petition; that therefore it is utterly impossible for anyone successfully to pass through the rites who is not already prepared to do so. It would be impossible — spiritually, intellectually, psychologically, and psychically — to initiate a beast into even the lowest of the initiatory grades, for the simple reason that the respective inner parts of its constitution are not yet functioning together under the direction and control of a self-conscious entity, as is the case with man.

It is upon this great and basic fact of natural fitness that reposes the entire structure of the ethical teaching which the great Masters of the past have given to their disciples. Discipline must precede the Mysteries — not by any Master's mandate, but simply because it is nature's irrefragable law. Man must prove himself to be worthy, and not only worthy but ready, and not only ready but fit, before his knocking at the portal of the sanctum sanctorum can be even heard; and remember that this "knock" is soundless and made without gesture, for it is a movement of the will, intense and determined, combined with an expanding of the consciousness.

How fit would a man be to enter into the dread regions of the Underworld and to face the often dangerous denizens of those realms if he cannot even control his emotional nature or successfully guide the operations of his own will, and if he does not understand the intricate functioning of his own consciousness? Again, how can a man pass safely through the regions of the superior realms of the universe, with what would be to him, in an unprepared state, all their manifold dangers and subtil appeals, if he himself is not already strong in will and expanded in consciousness and therefore fit to enter those realms? It would be as impossible as to ask a beast to take charge of a chemical laboratory or of an electrical works; or, on the other hand, to demand of a beast that it should compose an oratorio or write an outline of a cosmic philosophy that would mightily and persuasively sway the minds of men.

Yet hundreds of thousands, perhaps millions, of human beings today are not far from being ready and fit to undertake the first of the initiatory trials; but so sunken are they in the web and entanglements of material existence, that not only do they not know of these wonderful truths and of the powers lying latent and hid in their nature, but they would not care to attempt the tests even if they knew of the glorious possibilities that are their birthright. Their own ignorance and inertia prevent their advancing; and it is a part of our duty to awaken the minds of our fellow human beings and to open the doors of their hearts to nature's sublime verities.

I might say in passing that the greatest

and simplest preparation for all the various grades of initiation is our daily life. Here one can prove what he is made of; here he can show the stuff that is in him; here he can strengthen his character, evoke his will, enlarge his understanding, expand his heart-life. The Masters judge, or rather test, a beginner, a neophyte taking his first steps, by the way in which he acts in daily life and reacts to the temptations and trials that daily life puts upon him. These remarks, I repeat, are no vain words of an empty theory, but are sheer truth; and you will understand this at once when you remember that life is the great school, and that all the initiations, without a single exception, are but higher grades, the reaching of higher classes, in the school of life — life terrestrial and life cosmic.

Recollect the nature of the constitution of man which is composed of the following fundamentals or bases: first, a divinity derived from a star, the stellar parent for the individual, and each individual has his own. Next, a monadic essence of an intellectual type, called the mānasaputra, deriving from the sun. Third, a psychoemotional apparatus commonly called the human soul or monad, derivative from the moon-chain. And fourth, a psycho-vital-astral apparatus or body derivative from our own globe earth. And over all and within and running through all these is a superdivine, flameless fire of fundamental consciousness which we can generalize by calling it a son of the Boundless, whose habitat is the range of the frontierless spaces of space. This is man's own individual ladder of life; and he should earnestly and continuously strive with never an instant's intermission to raise his consciousness ever higher along this ladder, from and out of the body to place it in mastery of his psychomental lunar apparatus which he should conquer and control; and thence still higher to become at one with the mānasaputric essence living within him; and in future ages to arise out of this into something still more vast and lofty, which is the divine monad with its range of consciousness extending over the universe which we call the Galaxy or Milky Way; and later on, in aeons to come, he shall go higher, and then again higher, and still higher forever.

Thus verily are we born of the moon, children of the sun, offspring of the stars, and inheritors of the cosmic spaces; for space itself is we and we are it, for we and the Boundless are in essence not twain but one.

In these brief remarks I have endeavored to give, by hint and by allusion, some definite and clear ideas of the character and range of the matters comprised under the esoteric term, the initiation of the Great Renunciation. It too has its compensations unspeakably beautiful, and its end is the heart of the universe. Yet why do I say its "end"? This is but a figure of speech, but a manner of phrasing; for the heart of the universe is indeed boundless Infinitude, and the frontierless deeps of the Divine. Progress, therefore, is endless; the light becomes ever stronger as one progresses along the path; and what the chela would consider the loftiest summits of the Mystic East which he must climb, he finds when he has arrived and has placed his feet upon those distant peaks, that there are immeasurable distances still to go, and of a grandeur and sublimity which even the gods have not attained.

# IV

# Autumnal Equinox

## Autumnal Equinox

OF ALL the four sacred initiatory seasons of the year, none perhaps is so difficult to describe as the events and trials and success that belong to the initiation of the Autumnal Equinox, technically called the Great Passing. As the Winter Solstice is connected with the event called the Great Birth, and the Spring Equinox connected with the event technically called the Great Temptation, and the Summer Solstice with the sublime event called the Great Renunciation, so is the Autumnal Equinox connected with the event called the Great Passing, the recondite and in some cases dread mysteries of death.

As it has been pointed out, the Pratyeka Buddhas, great and holy men as they are, exemplify one aspect of the events belonging to the autumnal equinoctial initiation, for there comes a moment in the life cycle or esoteric history of a Pratyeka Buddha when he makes the final decision as between two paths that he must take: the one being to return among men as a Buddha of Compassion, or to advance steadily along the path of individual achievement for himself, with the light of eternity indeed shining upon his brow, but with his heart closed to the cry of misery and often of despair welling up from the multitudes of the struggling pilgrims on the path behind him.

The Pratyeka Buddha definitely chooses the Great Passing, dies absolutely, and for the term of a cosmic manvantara it may be, out of the world of men and sentient beings traveling behind him — and returns no more. He has become at one with his divine and spiritual parts, but in an enclosed and self-sufficient manner, so that although his being shines like the sun and he is sunken in the ineffable mystery and bliss of nirvana, his range of consciousness is limited to his own auric egg, widely spread or diffuse though this may be. There he remains plunged in the deeps of cosmic consciousness but, alas, oblivious of all except himself. Strange paradox, is it not, that though a part of the cosmic consciousness of the solar system, he realizes this and senses it only insofar as it pertains to his own perceiving essence.

Yet even the Pratyeka Buddha, by the very fact of his being and existing, exercises a steady although silent influence throughout the cosmic sphere of which he has become an integral albeit inactive part. Yet this influence is negative, not active, steady but diffuse; whereas the influence of the energies flowing forth from the heart of the being of a Buddha of Compassion is active, constructive, building, stimulating, and directly encouraging, by its vital fire.

The difference, as it is thus easily seen, between the Pratyeka Buddha and the Buddha of Compassion, is simply immense. The Buddhas of Compassion, like the Silent Watcher of our planetary chain of which they are the copies, renounce the unspeakable glories that the Great Passing confers, and become vibrant spiritual energies in the world's life and all that the world's life contains — energies vibrating with spiritual potencies, most of them too subtil to be described in words.

The Great Passing is the fourth and concluding initiation which every Master of Wisdom must go through, *and the glories of which he must renounce.* In this particular phase of the initiatory cycle leading to complete mahatmahood, the initiant must indeed, as in the preceding three initiations, pass through the Underworld; but in this, the fourth, the passage is but fleeting and is, as it were, like a traveler in a train rushing through scenes which have become familiar from other stoppings there; and instead of lingering in the Underworld, the energies are bent upon achieving cognizance of and intimate, individual acquaintanceship with, and indeed mastery of, the Upper Worlds.

Here then, in this initiation, are learned

all the intricate and very mysterious secrets connected with death, some of them sublimely beautiful, and some of them dreadful beyond any ordinary human imagination. The entire framework of the constitution of the initiant must be ruptured and torn apart for the time being, so that the divine monad may be utterly free and without shackles or trammels of any kind impeding its movements, to the end that it may ascend to and move among the starry spaces comprised within the encircling zone of our own stellar galaxy, our home-universe. There among the stars, and among the planets in orbital movement around those stars, must the freed divine monad of the initiant roam, free as a thought of a freed god, to become at one with — in stellar sphere after stellar sphere — all the different and differing phases and conditions not merely of stellar substance, but also of the cosmic consciousness.

To put the matter in other language, the divine monad returns to its own stellar parent and passes from star to star, ranging and wandering among them, familiarly and fully at home. What takes place in the case even of the ordinary human being when he dies, and which to such ordinary individual is blank unconsciousness because he has not evolved far enough to understand what he is undergoing, must to the freed divine monad of the master-initiant be made fully conscious and clear. Every phase of the process of death that takes place in ordinary human beings is undergone by the initiant at this time: sheath after sheath of the soul is dropped and abandoned, cast aside and for the time being forgotten, until the naked divinity stands alone, a living fire of energy in self-consciousness and self-cognizing memory.

Once that the shackles of the lower personal man, once that the enshrouding and crippling sheaths of the lower consciousness, have been cast off, then step by step, stair after stair, up the ladder of life, the monadic energy wings its lofty way. It must pass through every one of the twelve houses of the zodiac, the one after the other — or, if the words are better understood, undergo and experience the particular and peculiar influences flowing forth from each one of the twelve houses of the zodiac — until, when the round has been made and familiarity has been self-consciously achieved with what therein is, the descent begins, and downwards step by step, stair after stair, the hitherto freed monad clothes itself again with the sheaths of consciousness and with the various spiritual and ethereal and astral bodies that it had previously thrown off and forgotten. Finally, reaching our own earth again — the body lying entranced — it re-enters this world, raises its body anew and reappears among men, shining with a supernal light even more ethereal and marvelous and dread than that which clothes the successful initiant at the time of the rising from the trials of the Winter Solstice. The initiant has died, he has been dead in every sense of the word; but owing to the marvelous, magical processes and the protecting care and help of the great seers and sages who watch over and guard their younger brother, he is enabled to return from beyond the portals of death: he is literally "raised from the dead," and becomes a man again, but a man now glorified, sanctified, purified, in every part and portion of his composite constitution. He has passed beyond the portals of death, and has returned. He is fully reborn.

This is no case of renunciation as it is at the time of the Summer Solstice. The initiant is enabled to pass through these terrible trials precisely because the Great Renunciation had previously been made at the time of the initiation of the Summer Solstice, and he has gained the strength to die completely and fully and yet to return to human physical existence.

Just here, spiritually and ethically speaking, do we discern the difference between the Pratyeka Buddha who dies with a will, and dies gladly and joyfully for his own spiritual bliss, and the one who has made the Great Renunciation like the Buddhas of Compassion and their followers, who die indeed for the experience that it gives, for the great increase in knowledge that it brings with it, but who return to life in order to offer up themselves as a sacrifice in service to the world.

It is not easy to die completely. Men die daily, but imperfectly, at night when they lay themselves on their bed and fall asleep. But deliberate dying is a very difficult thing, for it is contrary to nature's customary law and processes. In any case, death is not immediate or sudden, not even in the case of the average man who dies. For long months preceding physical dissolution there is an adjustment for it which is an interior arrangement of the auric egg preparing the monadic parts for the postmortem peregrination. And at the end, for a short time preceding death, the consciousness hovers between earth and star, between the physical body and the sun, flashing sunwards and then back again a number of times, until finally the golden cord of life is ruptured, and unconsciousness — instant, immediate, and unspeakably sweet and soft — descends upon the dying, who thereafter is what men call dead.

I have hitherto been speaking of the fourth of the four grand initiations as it applies to the cases of the Great Ones who undergo it and who return among men; but there are the many other cases of those who take this initiation deliberately after the manner of the Pratyeka Buddhas and die from the world and return no more until aeons have passed and dropped one by one into the ocean of bygone time. These last are the cases of those who are on the way to becoming Pratyeka Buddhas, perhaps unknown to themselves, paradoxical as it may sound; and I doubt not that you would be astonished were you to realize how numerous are the human souls who crave the unspeakable peace and bliss of the nirvanic rest — clinging to life, longing for its continuance, they yet, strange paradox, choose the pathway of death.

The Great Ones undertake this fourth initiation in order to have firsthand experience in every respect, not only of the Underworld but more especially of the Upper Worlds, and of what every monad leaving incarnation must undergo in the ordinary course of dying.

In the initiation of the Winter Solstice the planets visited usually are the Moon, Venus, Mercury, and the Sun, and then there is a return; whereas in this fourth initiation of the Autumnal Equinox these same planets are passed through — during the process of what we may perhaps justly call a dissolution of the constitution — and the superior planets Mars, Jupiter, and Saturn, are likewise visited, and thence the freed monad wings its way outwards into the kosmic spaces. The return journey is made along the same pathway, and the sheaths or veils of consciousness that the monadic pilgrim dropped during these peregrinations in each one of the planets and in each one of the planes, are again picked up and reassumed, and thus the monadic ego clothes itself with its lower selves again and returns along the pathway by which it had ascended. The order of the planets as just above given must not be understood to be the order of the planets regularly followed.

It becomes obvious from the preceding teaching that man has in himself not only a physical or Earth-body, but a Lunar body, a Venusian body, a Hermetic or Mercurial body, a Solar body, a Martian body, a Jovian body, and a Saturnian body, as well as being clothed with the essences of kosmic space. Not only has man in his constitution these various planetary sheaths, but also his consciousness itself contains color-shades, as it were, or energies, or qualities, derivative from the various celestial bodies with which he is constitutionally in such strait and intimate union. This is the reason why the various bodies or elements of man's constitution are shed by the initiant as he traverses any one of these spheres, and why he must return to each one of the spheres in order to pick up such veil or sheath or clothing formerly shed, in order to become on earth once more a complete man. Man, therefore, as you see, is a child of the universe, composite of all its elements, and therefore is in very truth a microcosm, or little world. His very thought touches with ethereal fingers the most distant star, and the tiniest vibration of the most distant star has its reaction upon him.

Death, we may then see, in the majestic ceremonies of the fourth initiation of the autumnal equinoctial period, is but an ascension, a resurrection, out of certain grosser elements into elements much more ethereal; but the center of consciousness, the fiery spark of being, the monadic essence is a god, and remains untouched and unstained through the aeons, no matter what its children — which are its vehicles and sheaths of consciousness and inferior monads through which it works — do or undergo or suffer and enjoy.

Mark then, these two distinct but not conflicting elements of the teaching regarding the autumnal equinoctial initiation: (1)

All the greater initiants must pass through this initiation, but they return. They taste in it of death and vanquish it; and in the words of the Christian scripture they may say: "O death, where is thy sting? O grave, where is thy victory?" because the initiant rising successfully as an initiate has truly conquered death, and its mysteries in all their various phases are to him mysteries no longer. (2) The second element of the teaching is the fact that armies, multitudes, crowds, of human beings, at some time in their evolutionary pilgrimage, choose this initiation with deliberation for the sole purpose of passing out of the world and ken of men, to return no more. Such are the Pratyeka Buddhas, and those who, like them, prefer the bliss of individual nirvana to the self-sacrificing but sublime life and destiny of a Buddha of Compassion.

Remember this teaching in its elements. Try to carry the thoughts of it in your mind, for they are helpful and, when properly understood, the consciousness of these truths will wrap itself around you like a protecting buckler and shield. Or, to change the figure of speech, these teachings will become a light unto your feet, and will guide you along the path that humanity's greatest and noblest flowers of perfection have chosen to tread.